Thank you for Purchasing Sendo Coloring: Dogs Volume 1

Get 100 Print-Ready Coloring Pages

For Free

By signing up for our email list at:

https://mailchi.mp/f62281d0aeb7/sendo-coloring

Or by scanning the QR Code below

Check us out on Instagram at @sendocoloring to see more of our work

This Book
Belongs To

____

Affenpinscher

The Affenpinscher is a small dog breed that originated in Germany, typically sized at around 9-11 inches tall and weighing 7-9 pounds. They are also known as the "Monkey Dog" or "Monkey Pinscher" due to their monkey-like appearance and behaviour. They have a wiry, coarse coat that is typically black but can also be grey, silver, or black and tan and have a lifespan of about 12-15 years.

The Affenpinscher is known to be a loyal and affectionate companion, but can also be aloof with strangers, they are highly intelligent and can excel in obedience and agility training. But they are known to be independent and can be stubborn, which may make training difficult for inexperienced dog owners.

The Affenpinscher is a good choice for apartments or any type of small home living, as they do not require a lot of space. They are also known to be quite playful and energetic. Affenpinscher's make good watchdogs and are protective of their family.

The Affenpinscher is a member of the Terrier group but is not a true terrier. The breed was originally used to hunt rats and other small vermin on the farm. The breed was officially recognized by the AKC in 1936.

The Affenpinscher is a rare breed and may be difficult to find a reputable breeder. They require regular grooming to maintain their wiry coat. They are known to be good with other pets but may be aggressive towards other dogs if not socialized properly.

American Eskimo

The American Eskimo dog is a Spitz-type breed known for its thick, fluffy coat and pointed ears. Originally bred in Germany, this versatile breed excels in obedience and agility competitions. They come in three sizes: toy, miniature, and standard, and are highly trainable. American Eskimo dogs are known for their intelligence, loyalty, and affectionate nature.

They have thick coats that require regular grooming to maintain their appearance and prevent matting. They are generally healthy and have a lifespan of 12 to 15 years. The American Eskimo dog is a versatile breed that was originally bred for use as a watchdog and circus performer.

They have a compact and well-proportioned bodies with strong, muscular builds. American Eskimo dogs come in three sizes: toy, miniature, and standard. The toy size is under 9 inches tall, the miniature size is between 9 and 12 inches tall, and the standard size is between 15 and 19 inches tall.

American Eskimo dogs excel in obedience and agility competitions. They are protective and make good watchdogs, but can also be wary of strangers if not socialized properly. They are an active breed and require regular exercise to maintain their physical and mental well-being.

Due to their thick coat, American Eskimo dogs are well suited for cold climates, but can also tolerate warm weather if provided with shade and water. They are known for their ability to learn quickly. They have a high energy level, so they enjoy activities such as running, hiking, and playing fetch.

Dachshund

The Dachshund, also known as the "sausage dog," is a small, elongated breed with a distinct shape and personality. These cute and spunky dogs have been beloved by families for centuries and have become one of the most popular breeds in the world.

One of the first things that people notice about a Dachshund is their unique shape. They have long bodies and short legs, which gives them a low-to-the-ground appearance. This body shape was specifically bred for hunting small animals, such as badgers and foxes, in tight burrows. Despite their small size, Dachshunds are incredibly strong and athletic, and they have a natural hunting instinct.

Dachshunds come in two sizes: standard and miniature. Standard Dachshunds can weigh up to 32 pounds, while miniature Dachshunds weigh less than 11 pounds. They also come in a variety of coat types, such as smooth, wirehaired, and longhaired. Each coat type requires different grooming needs, but all Dachshunds have a tendency to shed.

Dachshunds are known for their lively and playful personalities. They are energetic and curious, and they have a strong desire to explore their surroundings. They can be stubborn and independent at times, but they are also very loyal and affectionate with their owners. Training and socialization are important to help them become well-behaved members of the family.

Due to their small size and elongated spine, Dachshunds are prone to certain health issues, such as intervertebral disc disease and obesity. Regular exercise, a healthy diet, and proper veterinary care can help prevent these issues and ensure that Dachshunds live long and healthy life.

One of the most endearing things about Dachshunds is their unique bark. They have a loud and distinctive bark that is easily recognizable. They also have a tendency to vocalize when they're excited or when they're trying to get their owners' attention. This can make them great watchdogs, but it can also be a nuisance if they're not properly trained.

Dachshunds have been popular pets for centuries and they have a rich history. They were originally bred in Germany in the 15th century and were used for hunting small game. They were brought to the United States in the late 19th century and have been a beloved companion breed ever since.

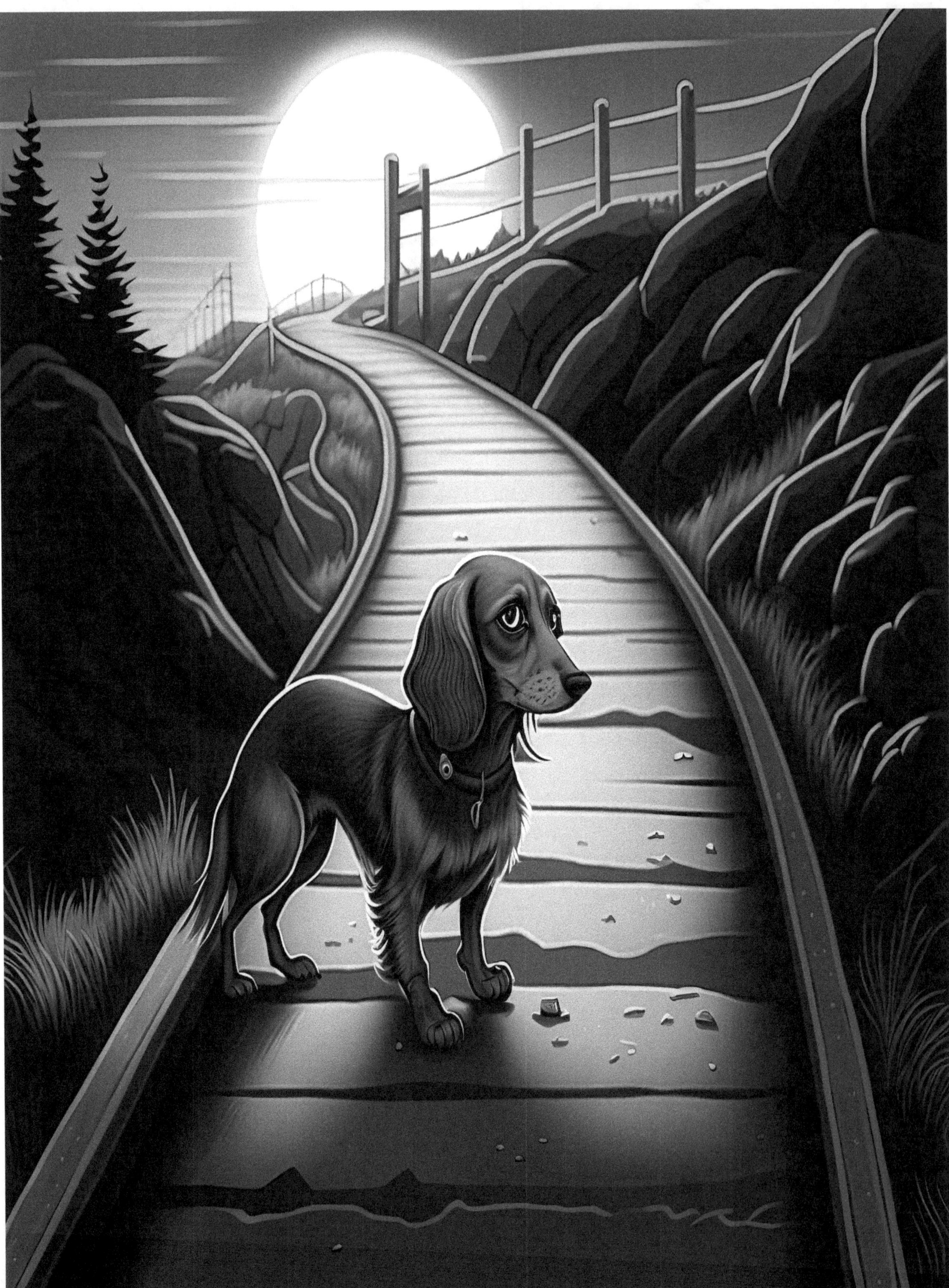

The Rottweiler is a powerful and majestic breed that has a strong and imposing appearance. They have a muscular build, a short and shiny black coat, and a confident and assertive presence. Rottweilers are known for their loyalty and protective nature and they are often considered one of the best guard dogs.

Rottweilers were originally bred in Germany as working dogs. They were used to herd cattle and pull carts, and they were also used as guard dogs for their owners' property. Their strength and endurance made them perfect for these tasks, and they were known for their ability to work hard and stay focused for long periods of time.

Rottweilers are large dogs, with males weighing between 110-130 pounds and females between 80-100 pounds. They have a strong and powerful appearance, with a broad head, a strong jaw, and a black coat that is short and shiny. They have a muscular build and a confident and assertive presence that commands respect.

Despite their intimidating appearance, Rottweilers are known for their loyalty and protective nature. They are highly protective of their family and will do whatever it takes to keep them safe. They are also known for their trainability, and with proper training, they can become well-behaved and obedient pets. They are also great with children and make loving and playful companions.

Rottweilers are highly active dogs, and they require regular exercise to maintain their physical and mental well-being. They are known for their endurance and stamina, and they enjoy activities such as running, hiking, and playing fetch. They also need regular training and mental stimulation to keep them stimulated and prevent boredom.

Due to their large size and powerful build, Rottweilers are prone to certain health issues such as hip dysplasia and bloat. Regular veterinary check-ups, a healthy diet, and proper exercise can help prevent these issues and ensure that Rottweilers live long and healthy life.

Rottweilers have a rich history and have been respected and valued for their strength and loyalty throughout the centuries. They were used as working dogs in ancient Rome and have been used as police and military dogs in modern times. They are also used as therapy and service dogs, as well as search and rescue dogs.

Airedale Terrier

The Airedale Terrier, also known as the "King of Terriers," is a large and spirited breed that has a strong and independent personality. They are known for their intelligence, confidence, and adaptability, making them one of the most versatile breeds in the world.

The Airedale Terrier is the largest of the terrier breeds, with males reaching heights of up to 23 inches and females up to 22 inches. They have a distinctive wiry, black and tan coat that requires regular grooming to maintain their appearance. They have a strong and athletic build, with a broad head and a long, bushy tail.

Airedale Terriers were originally bred in England to hunt small game, such as otters, and as a general-purpose farm dogs. They were known for their intelligence and trainability, and they quickly became popular with farmers and hunters. They were later used as police and military dogs, as well as search and rescue dogs.

Airedale Terriers are known for their intelligence and they excel in obedience and agility competitions. They have a strong desire to please their owners. With proper training and socialization, they can become well-behaved and obedient pets. They are also great with children and make loving and playful companions.

Airedale Terriers are highly active dogs and they require regular exercise to maintain their physical and mental well-being. They are known for their endurance and stamina, and they enjoy activities such as running, hiking, and playing fetch. They also need regular training and mental stimulation to keep them stimulated and prevent boredom.

Due to their large size and active nature, Airedale Terriers are prone to certain health issues such as hip dysplasia and bloat. Regular veterinary check-ups, a healthy diet, and proper exercise can help prevent these issues and ensure that Airedale Terriers live long and healthy life.

Airedale Terriers have a rich history and have been respected and valued for their intelligence, and adaptability throughout the centuries. They have been used as police and military dogs, search and rescue dogs, and therapy and service dogs. They are also known to be great hunting and farm dogs.

Bichon Frisé

The Bichon Frisé, also known as the "curly lap dog," is a small and playful breed that has a distinctive fluffy and curly coat. They have a cheerful and affectionate personalities and have become one of the most popular breeds for families and individuals alike.

The Bichon Frisé is a small breed, weighing 7-12 pounds, and standing 9-12 inches tall. They have a distinctive fluffy and curly coat that comes in white or cream color. They have round heads, dark expressive eyes, and fluffy tail . Their coat requires regular grooming to maintain its appearance, including regular brushing and clipping.

Bichon Frisé was originally bred as circus dogs in Mediterranean countries and were later used as companion animals. They were known for their cheerful and affectionate personalities and were particularly popular with sailors and traders, who would take them on long voyages.

Bichon Frisé are known for their cheerful and affectionate personality. They are highly sociable and love to be around people, are great with children and make loving and playful companions.

Bichon Frisé is also known for being low-shedding and hypoallergenic, making them a good choice for people with allergies. They are highly adaptable and can do well in both small apartments and large houses, as long as they get enough exercise and mental stimulation.

Great Dane

The Great Dane, also known as the "Apollo of Dogs" due to its majestic appearance and regal bearing, is a breed that is known for its impressive size and elegant appearance. With its tall, lean build and long, flowing coat, the Great Dane is a sight to behold.

The Great Dane is a gentle giant, known for its calm and friendly disposition. These dogs are great with children and make excellent family pets. They are also known for their loyalty and protective nature, making them great guard dogs. Despite their size, Great Danes are very docile and easy to train. They are also known for their intelligence and are eager to please, making them a great breed for first-time dog owners.

The Great Dane's origins can be traced back to ancient times, with evidence of similar breeds depicted in Egyptian and Greek artwork. The breed was officially recognized in the late 1800s in Germany, where it was used primarily as a hunting dog. However, over time, the breed's purpose shifted to more of a companion and show dog.

The Great Dane's coat is short and smooth and comes in a variety of colors including black, blue, fawn, harlequin, mantle, and merle. The most common color is black. Grooming for a Great Dane is minimal, with regular brushing to remove dead hair and nail clipping as needed. They are an average shedder.

One of the most striking features of the Great Dane is its size. These dogs can reach up to 34 inches in height at the shoulder and weigh up to 200 pounds. Despite their size, Great Danes are surprisingly agile and are known for their graceful movements. They are also known for their endurance and can keep up with the most active families. The Great Dane has a lifespan of around 6-8 years

Afghan Hound

The Afghan Hound is a majestic and elegant dog breed known for its distinctive long, silky coat and regal bearing. This ancient breed hails from the high mountains of Afghanistan, where it was used as a hunting and guard dog by nomadic tribes. The Afghan Hound is a sight to behold, with its unique and striking appearance, making it one of the most recognizable dog breeds in the world.

The Afghan Hound is a large breed, standing around 29 inches tall at the shoulder and weighing around 60 pounds. Their coat is comes in a variety of colors including black, cream, gold, red, silver and white. The coat is thick and requires regular grooming to keep it in top condition. Their long hair around their ears, chest and legs is particularly striking and makes them stand out in a crowd.

The Afghan Hound is a very independent and aloof breed. They are known for their reserved nature and can be somewhat stand-offish with strangers. However, they are very loyal and affectionate with their families and make great companions for those who understand their unique personalities. They have a strong prey drive, and if not trained well they may chase small animals.

Despite their independent nature, the Afghan Hound is a highly trainable breed. They are intelligent and eager to please, but training should be done with patience and consistency. They excel in agility and obedience training. Socializing them from an early age will make them more comfortable with new people and environments. They are also known for having a short lifespan of around 10-12 years.

The Afghan Hound has a rich history and is steeped in legend and mystery. They were highly valued by nomadic tribes for their hunting skills and were also believed to have mystical powers. The breed was first introduced to the Western world in the late 1800s, and since then, has become a popular show dog and beloved companion.

Alaskan Malamute

The Alaskan Malamute is a large, powerful and majestic dog breed that originated in the Arctic regions of Alaska. These dogs were bred by the Mahlemut Inuit tribe to be hardworking and strong, able to pull heavy loads through the snow and ice.

The Alaskan Malamute is known for its thick, fluffy coat, which helps to keep it warm in the harsh Arctic climate. The Alaskan Malamute stands at around 25 inches tall at the shoulder and can weigh up to 85 pounds.

They have a thick coat that comes in a variety of colors including gray, black, sable, and white. Their coat requires regular grooming to keep it in top condition, as they shed heavily twice a year. They have a thick undercoat that keeps them warm and a coarse outer coat that protects them from the elements.

The Alaskan Malamute is a friendly, outgoing and playful breed. They are known for their affectionate nature and love to be around their family. They are great with children and other pets and make excellent family pets. However, they have a strong pack instinct and require a confident and experienced owner who can establish themselves as the leader of the pack.

The Alaskan Malamute is an active and energetic breed that requires a lot of exercise and mental stimulation. They were bred to pull heavy loads and as such, they have a lot of energy to burn. They excel in activities such as weight pulling, sledding and skijoring. They also make great hiking and running companions. It's important to provide them with plenty of opportunities to burn off their energy to prevent destructive behavior.

The Alaskan Malamute is a relatively healthy breed, but, like all breeds, they are prone to certain health issues. Some of the health concerns include hip dysplasia, bloat, and eye problems. Regular vet checkups and a healthy diet can help to mitigate these risks. They have a lifespan of around 12-15 years.

The Alaskan Malamute has a rich history as a working dog and has played an important role in the lives of the Mahlemut tribe. They were used for hunting, herding, and as a means of transportation in the harsh Arctic climate. Today, the Alaskan Malamute is still a popular working dog and is also a beloved companion.

www.ingramcontent.com/pod-product-compliance
Lightning Source LLC
LaVergne TN
LVHW080359180826
845678LV00026B/2034
9798373965460